The Book of Knights

by Julia March

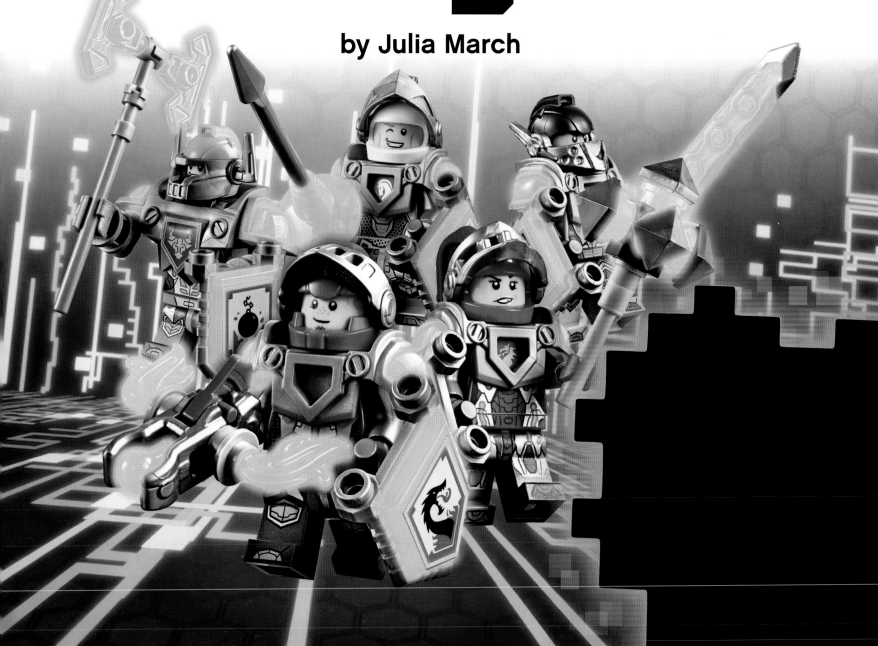

CONTENTS

DEFENDING THE KINGDOM

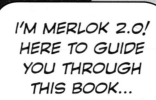

FIND ME ON PAGE 11!

I'M MERLOK 2.0! HERE TO GUIDE YOU THROUGH THIS BOOK...

INTRODUCTION

Greetings, young knights! I'm Merlok the magician, but I'm afraid you've caught me at a bad time.

Our beautiful kingdom of Knighton is being menaced by an evil jester and a gang of fiery monsters called Magma Monsters. They're escaping from a talking magic book, the Book of Monsters (it isn't my fault, OK?). Five newly trained knights are out there battling the monsters, and I'm busy uploading digital NEXO Powers to their shields to help them. But it's touch and go as to whether we'll save Knighton.

We could use all the help we can get. Interested? Then read on...

By the way, sorry if I'm a bit bright, but I'm stuck in this computer system, and I'm now a hologram (here's a picture of how I looked when I was a normal magician).

MERLOK

Famous for defeating Knighton's evil wizards long ago, this much-loved magician was sucked into a computer system after a magical explosion. He soon returned as Merlok 2.0—a hologram magician who uploads amazing digital powers to the five knights. That's digi-magic!

THE KNIGHTS OF KNIGHTON

Prepare to meet the five bravest knights in all of Knighton! Lance, Aaron, Axl, Macy, and Clay have just graduated from Knights' Academy and are ready to take on anything... well, they may need a little help from their friends first.

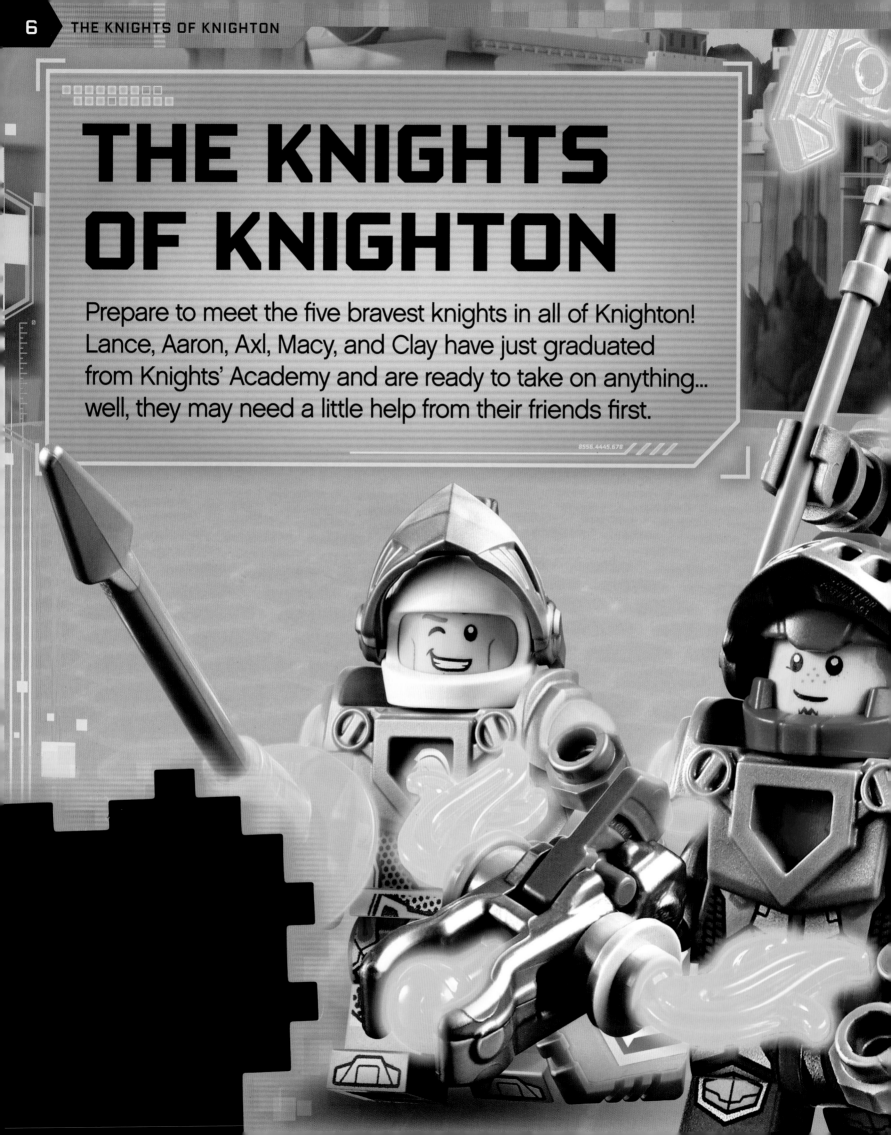

CLAY MOORINGTON

No knight trains harder than Clay Moorington. He rarely stops. If you see him out of his armor and in front of a screen, don't assume he's chilling out. Nope. He'll be watching a training video, and planning team tactics!

Clay's **armor** has been strengthened to withstand heat, monster attack, and blows from weapons.

HEY! WHERE IS EVERYONE? IT'S TRAINING TIME!

The **rising falcon** is Clay's personal crest.

Total recall
Clay has memorized the Knight's Code. Talent, bravery, and dedication have made Clay a star pupil.

Protective armor extends to **knee pads**.

CLAY'S SWORD

This single-handed claymore is Clay's favorite weapon. It is nearly as tall as Clay and super-heavy, too, but he wields it like a pro. It must be a result of all those hours spent in strength training!

Double-edged blade

NEXO Powers infuse knights with extra powers to battle monsters—and give weapons their glow

CLAY'S HOVER HORSE

If you think horses are old-fashioned, think again! Clay's Hover Horse is a high-tech flying machine, perfect for speeding after monsters. Saddle up, and hold on tight!

Saddle holds one knight—sitting or standing

Blue head coloring unique to Clay's horse

Clay's shield, upgraded to show Giant Growth NEXO Power, slots onto the side

Rear booster provides an extra blast of energy

HEROIC HOPES

Clay is an orphan from Dnullib—the smallest, dullest village in Knighton. His humble start to life has made him eager to prove himself. His bravery is tested when he comes face to fiery face with a monster in Merlok's library!

CLAY IS GOOD AT EVERYTHING— EXCEPT HAVING A *SENSE OF HUMOR!*

CLAY'S RUMBLE BLADE

When this vehicle rumbles, monsters tumble! Clay's Rumble Blade is a six-wheeled tank with a sword-shaped front. Even better—it's actually four magnificent monster-busting machines in one—with plenty of cool features to help Clay and his Squire Bots.

DATA FILE

SET NUMBER: 70315
PARTS: 514
RELEASED: 2016
MINIFIGURES: 4

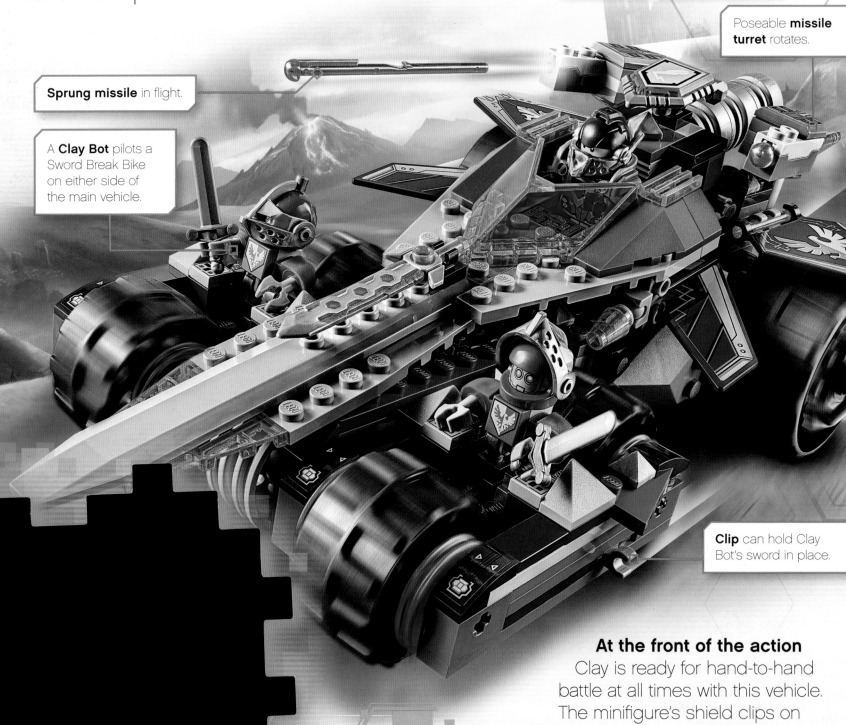

Poseable **missile turret** rotates.

Sprung missile in flight.

A **Clay Bot** pilots a Sword Break Bike on either side of the main vehicle.

Clip can hold Clay Bot's sword in place.

At the front of the action
Clay is ready for hand-to-hand battle at all times with this vehicle. The minifigure's shield clips on behind the cockpit, and his claymore sword in front of it.

BLADE FLYER

There's something in the air... it's Clay in his Sword Speeder, fighting his foes above the ground. This fast flyer, with its twin blasters, lifts off from the base vehicle. It resembles a giant, flying version of Clay's sword.

Clay's claymore sword clipped to front

Speeder exhaust

Rapid-fire blasters on front of wing

Button to release Sword Break Bikes

Bike is compact one-seater

SWORD BREAK BIKES

At the press of a button, two Sword Break Bikes detach from the Rumble Blade, and hurtle into battle. They're usually piloted by loyal Clay Bots, but fellow knights Macy and Axl have been known to hop aboard!

RUMBLE BASE

This three-wheeled vehicle is the heart of the Rumble Blade. It has two high-tread rear wheels that eat up rough terrain. Up top are two missile turrets that can be raised, lowered, and rotated in all directions.

DID YOU KNOW?

Clay's signature power is called the "Stronghold of Resolution." When he strikes the ground he can summon a falcon to rise up and attack the enemy.

OK, CLAY... LET'S GO GET THOSE MONSTERS! READY TO RUMBLE?

AARON FOX

Being a knight is all about the thrills for Aaron Fox. He's a born risk-taker. Show him something tall and he'll climb it. Show him something fast and he'll race it. Problem is, he often races *into* things without really thinking about it. And that can lead to trouble!

DID YOU KNOW?

Aaron's signature power is called "Swift Sting." Armed with this power, Aaron launches bouncing projectiles at the enemy—creating chaos with every bound!

Fox rocks!

Aaron loves rock 'n' roll music. In battle, he often snaps into "Music Mode," strumming his Blazer Bow like an electric guitar as arrows fly out.

Orange fox is Aaron's family crest—and surname, too!

OH C'MON! WHAT COULD GO WRONG?

Aaron just hopped off this **hover shield** five seconds ago!

Blazer Bow energy bolt loaded and ready to fly.

Aaron's **signature color** is green.

AARON'S HOVER HORSE

LIke the other knighs, Aaron rides a high-tech Hover Horse into battle. Unlike the other heroes, Aaron doesn't know the meaning of "Whoah!." He and his Hover Horse will charge straight into the thick of battle without a plan.

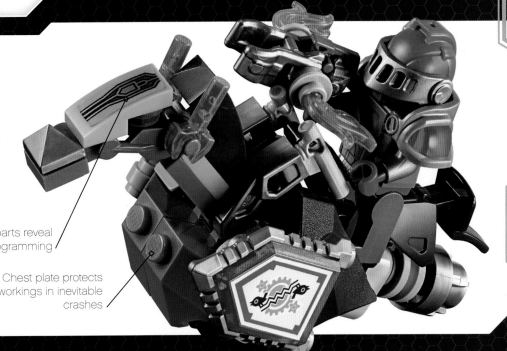

Exposed parts reveal advanced programming

Chest plate protects workings in inevitable crashes

BLAZER BOWS

To get good thrills, you need good skills. Aaron trains hard at target practice, and is a crack shot with his Blazer Bow. Actually, Aaron can fire almost any kind of bow. He owns several variations of his signature bow, and has even asked his inventor friend Robin to build him a giant bow so that he can fire himself across Knighton!

Energy bolts release when trigger is pulled

Blazer Bow version 1

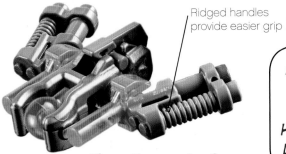

Ridged handles provide easier grip

Blazer Bow version 2

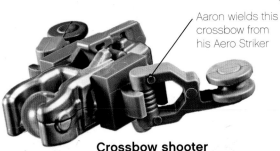

Aaron wields this crossbow from his Aero Striker

Crossbow shooter

HOVER SHIELD

Aaron's shield doesn't just protect him in battle. He also uses it as a hoverboard to get around Knighton in super-fast time. Traveling this way is fun, and also reminds Aaron of surfing at the beach in his seaside hometown of Grindstead.

I'D TELL AARON TO BE MORE CAREFUL... IF HE'D HOLD STILL LONG ENOUGH!

AARON'S AERO STRIKERS

Head's up! Aaron's Aero Strikers are ready for action. These awesome flying vehicles are just as speedy as their adrenaline fueled owner. The Aero Striker V2 is the biggest flyer—with room for an extra Squire Bot to come along for the ride. It is equipped with multiple missiles to fire at meddling monsters.

DATA FILE

SET NUMBER: 70320
PARTS: 301
RELEASED: 2016
MINIFIGURES: 3

Aaron Bot copilot sits in the back.

Crossbow shooter mounted on wing.

Wing mounted **shooter** can swivel.

Forward blasters aimed by Aaron at the controls.

Large engines for powerful flight.

Speedy Striker

The Aero Striker V2's aerodynamic shape and two huge engines allow the high-tech vehicle to reach super-sonic speeds. The wings feature Aaron's fox insignia, and his familiar green coloring.

SECRET WEAPON

If the Magma Monsters think all they have to worry about is dodging the Aero Striker V2's missiles, they should think again! When Aaron needs to get closer to the action, he can blast off on his own mini flyer, leaving his Aaron Bot copilot to take over flying the Aero Striker V2.

Mini flyer slots into these grooves when docking

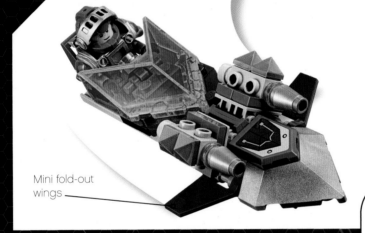

Mini fold-out wings

FLYING SOLO

Aaron's mini flyer is shaped like an arrow, allowing it to slice through the air with ease. The sharp point at the front also wards off flying monsters. Two blasters mounted on the front add firepower, and two fold-out wings allow the flyer to glide smoothly. Whee!

I ALWAYS KNEW AARON WOULD TURN OUT TO BE A HIGH FLYER!

ALTERNATIVE FLYER

The knights are never short of cool gadgets. Aaron's other flyer, the Aero Striker V1 is a small but powerful flyer loaded with a single missile and two sharp blades.

Missile in flight

MACY HALBERT

Some princesses love palace life, with all its royal duties. Not Macy! She longs to be out there swinging her mace and battling monsters. Macy's mom, Queen Halbert, thinks that's cool. She used to be a warrior herself.

DID YOU KNOW?

Macy's signature power is "Rushing Strike." Armed with this NEXO Power, Macy can charge headlong with strength at enemies before they know what's coming.

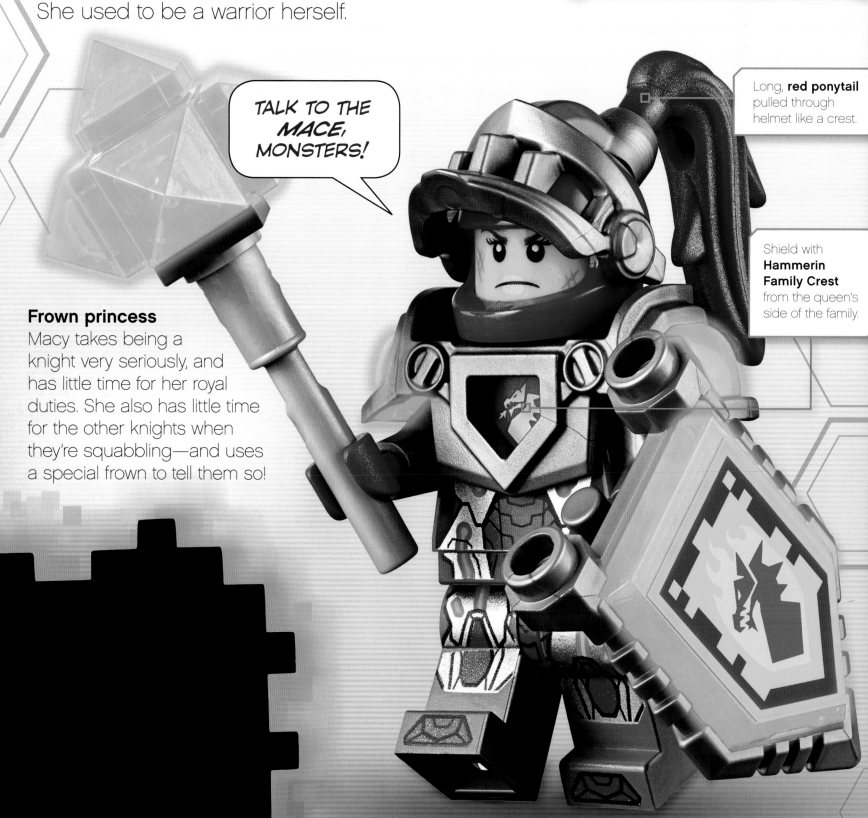

TALK TO THE *MACE,* MONSTERS!

Frown princess
Macy takes being a knight very seriously, and has little time for her royal duties. She also has little time for the other knights when they're squabbling—and uses a special frown to tell them so!

Long, **red ponytail** pulled through helmet like a crest.

Shield with **Hammerin Family Crest** from the queen's side of the family.

ROYAL ARGUMENT

King Halbert wants Macy to be happy, but only if she's doing nice, safe things such as hosting palace feasts. When Macy graduates from Knights' Academy, he won't give her the shield that would make her an official knight—to Macy's displeasure!

MACY'S PHOTON MACES

Macy's powered-up Photon Mace can send any monster it touches scurrying back into the Book of Monsters, and also deflects incoming missiles. Wielding this power weapon demands strength and agility. Macy practices daily with punching bags.

Power Mace has a good swing and gives electrical shocks

Bright red coloring acts as a warning to monsters

Thicker, heavier spikes

Power Mace   **The Hama Mace**   **Ultimate Mace**

MACY'S HOVER HORSE

If she wanted, Macy could ride a royal horse covered in jewels. But that wouldn't be practical for fighting monsters. Macy prefers her Hover Horse, which she controls with one hand while gripping her mace in the other.

Aerial receivers shaped like ears

WHEN IT COMES TO MACE-FIGHTING, MACY TAKES THE CROWN!

MACY'S THUNDER MACE

Princess Macy always knows how to make an entrance, and she's ready to roll in her awesome Thunder Mace. With its flip-up rotating cannons and huge front wheel, this mammoth motorcycle is a force to be reckoned with.

Rotating cannon with space for six missiles.

Separate **cockpit** for Squire Bot.

Tinted windshield protects Macy in the cockpit.

Front wheel swerves left or right to steer.

Shield **storage point** and **charger**.

Shield charger

Macy can recharge her shield at the shield storage point, leaving her hands free to steer.

DATA FILE

SET NUMBER: 70319
PARTS: 202
RELEASED: 2016
MINIFIGURES: 3

FLIP-UP CANNONS

When not in use, the two rotating cannons fold neatly down beside the cockpit. At the flick of a switch, they flip up into position at the back of the Thunder Mace, ready to launch a surprise attack on marauding Magma Monsters.

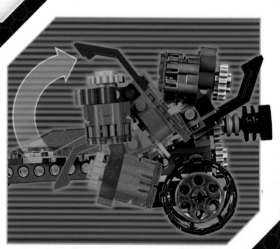

MACY'S MACE SLAMMER

For some missions, Macy needs a smaller, speedier way to get around. Her Mace Slammer is a miniature, but highly efficient, armored flyer, tough enough for any battle. With more than one vehicle at her disposal, Macy is equipped for any occasion.

DATA FILE

SET NUMBER: 70323
PARTS: 1186
RELEASED: 2016
MINIFIGURES: 8

Macy steers with the **control stick**.

Jet engine gives speed.

Packing light
This small flyer has just enough room for Macy in the cockpit. Her shield and mace can be stored on the sides.

Armored wings add protection.

Air vents keep the engine cool.

One of two **flick missiles**.

Missile under wing

Ball shooter

HIDDEN MISSILES

The Mace Slammer is packed with hidden ammo—missiles hidden beneath the jet's wings and a ball shooter tucked under its nose. Macy is just full of surprises!

THESE VEHICLES ARE NOTHING SHORT OF A-MACE-ING!

Twin-headed **battle-ax**.

AXL

This gentle giant has no last name. What he does have is an appetite... for battle, food, and music. When the foe is beaten and dinner's eaten, Axl strums the electric lute with his band, the Boogie Knights.

Extra-large **suit of armor** fits snugly. Axl rarely removes it, he loves being a knight so much.

Axl's **unique helmet** resembles a bull's head with horns.

IS THAT THE LUNCH BELL? MUSIC TO MY EARS!

Big surprise
Axl is from the hill country. His ancestors may once have been dwarves, and his shorter-sized family was surprised when their boy ate and ate... and grew and grew!

Axl's family crest shows a **bull insignia**.

Axl's shield shows his Signature Power, Raging Rally, which allows him to heal in battle.

FOOD FAN

Can anyone hear a rumbling noise? It's not the sound of a distant battle; it's just Axl's tummy. He's *always* hungry! Chef Eclair is teaching Axl to cook (in extra-large portions), and Axl was pleased with how this soufflé turned out—until he was summoned for training and it collapsed!

AXL'S HOVER HORSE

Heavyweight heroes need steeds with maximum horsepower. Axl's Hover Horse may look like the others, but it has been strengthened to handle his burly bulk.

Axl's helmet is yellow—his favorite color

Extra-large handelbars

Wall Block power creates a rising stone wall

I PREDICT BIG THINGS FOR THIS KNIGHT. REALLY BIG THINGS!

AXL'S AXES

Chopping, slicing, crushing, mashing... Axl can do all these things with his array of axes. And that means on the battlefield as well as in the kitchen.

Single-bladed variant

Dual-bladed battle-ax

Long-handled battle-ax

AXL'S TOWER CARRIER

When a knight towers over everyone else on the battlefield, he needs a vehicle that does the same. And for once, Axl seems more focused on beating the enemy than eating snacks. His Tower Carrier is kitted out with a host of impressive features, including a catapult, two missile launchers, and a disk shooter, plus a detachable tower.

DATA FILE

SET NUMBER: 70322
PARTS: 670
RELEASED: 2016
MINIFIGURES: 4

Covered **control room** for Axl Bot.

Battering ram clears a path ahead.

CATAPULT

The tower hides a secret weapon—a catapult! The catapult swivels on an axis, and folds out when the tower is removed.

Catapult bucket large enough to launch missiles

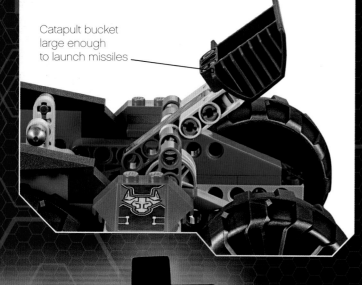

Carrier   Tower

TWO IN ONE

As well as providing a vantage point from which to aim weapons, the tower has wheels of its own and can detach from the carrier to form a second vehicle.

Laser cannon and **spring-loaded shooters**.

Axl sits in the **cockpit**.

Detachable **tower** hides catapult.

Disk shooter mounted on tower to increase **range**.

Rugged, rolling all-terrain **wheels**.

Sides feature Axl's **bull insignia**.

All-terrain wheels

BATTLE TOWER

Once detached, the tower forms an impressive battle station, from which Axl can fire an arsenal of weapons. The laser cannon and spring-loaded shooters turn up and down on two arms.

DID YOU KNOW?

In its siege-battle form, Axl's Tower Carrier is perfect for taking on and attacking enemy castle locations such as Jestro's Volcano Lair.

Room to spare

Axl and his Axl Bot can store extra weapons and tools in four secret compartments under the wheel flaps. There is also a vault under the tower to store any Magic Books that Axl finds.

AXL-ENT WORK, AXL. I MEAN, EXCELLENT. AHEM.

LANCE RICHMOND

Rich, handsome, and popular, Lance parties in the trendiest knight clubs and sports the flashiest armor. Spoiled? Yes, but he's a good guy at heart. He just needs to learn that sometimes you have to work hard to get things.

Shiny armor he can see his face in (and he likes what he sees!).

Long, **pointy lance** keeps monsters at bay.

Flared hilt helps to protect Lance's arm and chest.

OK FANS... AUTOGRAPHS AFTER MY NAP!

Richmond family crest features a **horse insignia**.

Rich Kid

Lance is from Auremville and one of Knighton's wealthiest families. His privileged position can lead him to lazily leave his Squire Bot, Dennis, to do everything for him.

LANCE'S LANCES

With no money worries, Lance is often seen in fancy stores splashing his cash on pricey gadgets and weapons. His collection of high-tech lances is his pride and joy—and he even named them after his nannies!

Clean white design is pretty, but not so practical!

Jousting-style lance is lightweight for use from Hover Horse.

Randi
Simple design is Lance's fall-back weapon.

Helle

Heidi
Streamlined design means lances can be moved swiftly.

Hanne

FIGHT KNIGHTS

Clay thinks that Lance doesn't take the Knight's Code seriously, and says so. Lance tells Clay to chill out. As they clash in the training arena, Clay finds Lance to be a tougher opponent than he expects. Maybe Lance has been taking his training seriously after all?

LANCE'S HOVER HORSE

This horse-shaped vehicle may lack hooves, but it goes at a gallop thanks to high-speed hover technology. Fast, nippy, and powerful, it's one charged-up charger! Lance calls it his "stallion."

Steering unit instead of reins

Neck straining eagerly toward the action!

AH, LANCE! SO TALENTED. SO BOLD. SO STYLISH. SO... ER... LAZY!

LANCE'S MECHA HORSE

Every knight needs a horse, but for Lance it has to be strictly high-tech. Feeding? Watering? Grooming? Not Lance's thing. He prefers his mount to be metal. Lance has named his Mecha Horse Concordo, and with its shiny blue coat and stamping hooves, it's just right for a knight-about-town. Ride on!

Heidi lance can be stored at the side.

Orange mane acts as a handy windshield, while head and neck can move in unison, or flex individually.

DATA FILE

SET NUMBER: 70312
PARTS: 237
RELEASED: 2016
MINIFIGURES: 3

Hooves can rotate for greater, more agile movement.

High horse
The Mecha Horse is tall, and when it's in "rear" mode it looks even more impressive. It also gives Lance a few extra feet to look down on his monster opponents. That gives him a horse-sized kick!

Hinged legs move as a single unit.

TURBO JOUSTER

In its alternative form, the Mecha Horse is still called Concordo, but becomes a sweet and swift low rider motorcycle also known as the Turbo Jouster. Lance switches to the Jouster when he wants to speed right down into the heart of the action. Actually, he sometimes switches to the Jouster just to impress his fans.

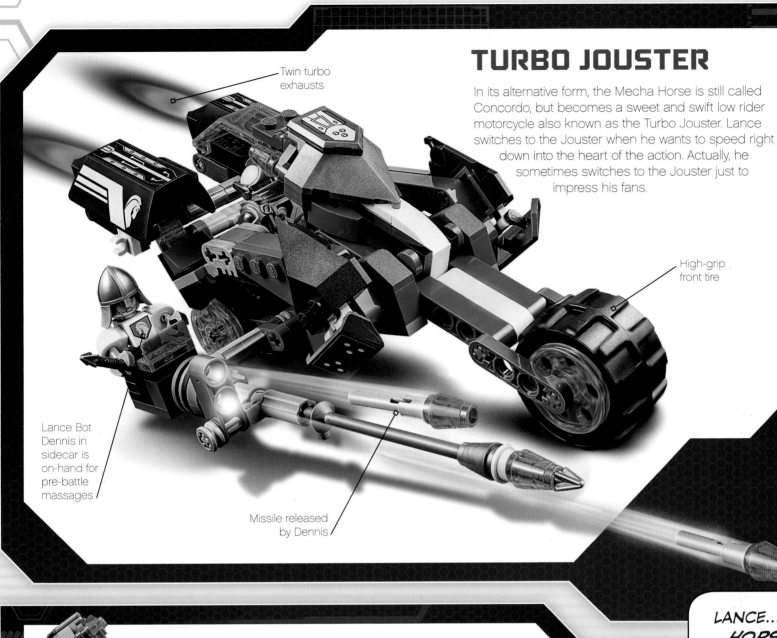

Twin turbo exhausts

High-grip front tire

Lance Bot Dennis in sidecar is on-hand for pre-battle massages

Missile released by Dennis

HORSE TRADING

Time to trade your hooves for some flashy wheels? It's easy with Lance's Mecha Horse. The shiny steed simply folds up, transforming into the powerful Turbo Jouster bike in seconds.

Hinged legs fold up, and front legs fold flat

Mecha Horse mode

Wheel swings forward as head moves back

Turbo Joust mode

LANCE... STOP *HORSING AROUND* AND CONCENTRATE!

SQUIRE BOTS

Every knight needs a Squire Bot! These small, robotic helpers wait on the knights, performing day-to-day tasks and providing backup on the battlefield. In Knighton, a Squire Bot is a knight's best friend.

Visor on helmet lifts to reveal this Clay Bot's toothy face.

Clay Bot

Like his master, Clay's Squire Bot is honest and eager. Unlike his master, his Clay Bot is a bit dim and is often getting his orders mixed up!

Armor in **Clay's color**—bright blue.

SIRE... I'VE SHARPENED YOUR BOOTS!

DID YOU KNOW?

Squire Bots have limited intelligence, and can often be seen talking to toasters. Some keep them as pets, or talk to them as if they are siblings.

Curved hands can hold either tools or weapons.

ROYAL BOTS

These little fellows are proud to serve King and Queen Halbert. There are several of them—it takes a lot of work to run a castle—and their helmets and faces vary. Some are Royal Soldiers, whose job is to defend the kingdom. Others are King Bots, who are more like butlers and domestic servants.

King Halbert's royal lion crest

Axl Bot

Axl is a laid-back guy, so his Squire Bot must have an easy time, right? Wrong! He's constantly running around bringing snacks, snacks, and more snacks for Axl.

Axl's Squire Bot carries a miniature ax

All Squire Bots wear heavy black boots

Lance Bot

Lance can be a bit lazy so his Squire Bot Dennis doesn't get much rest. Yet in between armor-shining and massage-giving, he still finds time to make sure Lance minds his manners.

Aaron Bot

Keeping up with thrill-seeking Aaron isn't easy, and this Squire Bot isn't always sure where his master has gone. He just hovers around waiting for Aaron to return on his hover shield.

Tunic emblazoned with Aaron's crest

I'M PRINCESS MACY'S BOT-IN-WAITING!

Macy Bot

Macy's Squire Bot tries to be as brave as Macy is. She even tries to look like Macy. A Bot can't grow a ponytail, so she wears a red plume on her helmet instead.

CHEF ECLAIR

This Chef Bot is always on fire! He loves cooking up something tasty, either in the castle or in the Fortrex kitchen. Needless to say, Axl thinks Chef Eclair is the best Bot in the world (next to his own!).

THERE ARE BOTS OF LOTS... I MEAN LOTS OF BOTS IN KNIGHTON.

AVA PRENTIS

Ava is in her first year at Knights' Academy, but she's already a tech whiz. Who found Merlok 2.0 in the castle's computer system? Who is tidying his files to find access to his old spells? Ava, that's who.

Dear diary
Nobody knows it, but Ava is a bit of a romantic. She keeps a secret diary where she records all of her innermost thoughts.

> LET'S SEE IF I CAN "MAGIC" A SOLUTION THAT ACTUALLY WORKS.

Clip for **gadget-bag** strap.

AVA'S GAMEPAD

In her downtime, Ava can still be found with her eyes glued to a screen. Gaming is another of her many talents.

DIGITAL MAGIC

At first, Ava thinks magic is outdated, and technology is the only way to go. But working with Merlok 2.0 brings a magical mash-up of her skills and those of the kooky wizard's. The result is a powerful new digital magic.

ROBIN UNDERWOOD

This impatient young page is also a freshman at Knights' Academy. The son of the castle maintenance man, Robin has a fierce talent for building and fixing things. That's good news for the knights!

> WHY CAN'T I BE A KNIGHT RIGHT NOW?

Robin is no **chicken**, this insignia is simply the Underwood family crest.

Boy builder

Robin loves building amazing weapons and gadgets for the knights. His repertoire extends as far as building massive Mechs and Ultimate Armor variants.

MINI FORTREX

When the knights need to redesign a rolling castle to turn it into a high-tech base, Robin is only too happy to help. He even builds himself a Mini Fortrex, complete with missile launcher!

Mini drawbridge

> PATIENCE, BOY! IT TAKES TIME TO... HEHEH... *BUILD* A CAREER AS A KNIGHT.

KING AND QUEEN HALBERT

King Halbert is a mellow monarch, who just wants peace, love, and tournaments. Queen Halbert is an ex-knight from a warrior village, who can still wield a mean hammer if she has to. Opposites really do attract!

LOOK, I DON'T WANT TO FIGHT, BUT...

Golden sword hilt is an old remnant of the ancient royal Halbert Sword.

Gold battle armor is suitable for royalty.

Queen Halbert prefers her head to be **crown-free** (it's so *heavy*!).

FANCYPANTS

The knights have Squire Bots and so too does the king. Mr. Fancypants acts as advisor to the royal couple—greeting dignitaries, preventing disasters, checking His Majesty is well fed...

King Halbert
Why does his daughter want to go out and fight monsters? The King doesn't understand it—until the monsters turn up at the castle. Then he realizes that sometimes it's right to fight.

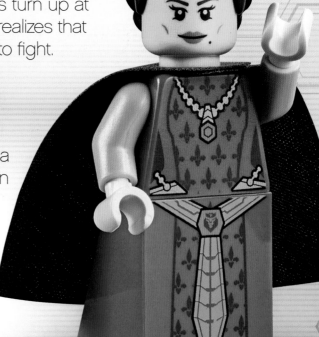

Queen Halbert
Hama Halbert is from a warrior family in eastern Knighton. She almost always takes Macy's side when Macy argues with the king about being a knight (although she does it in the nicest possible way!).

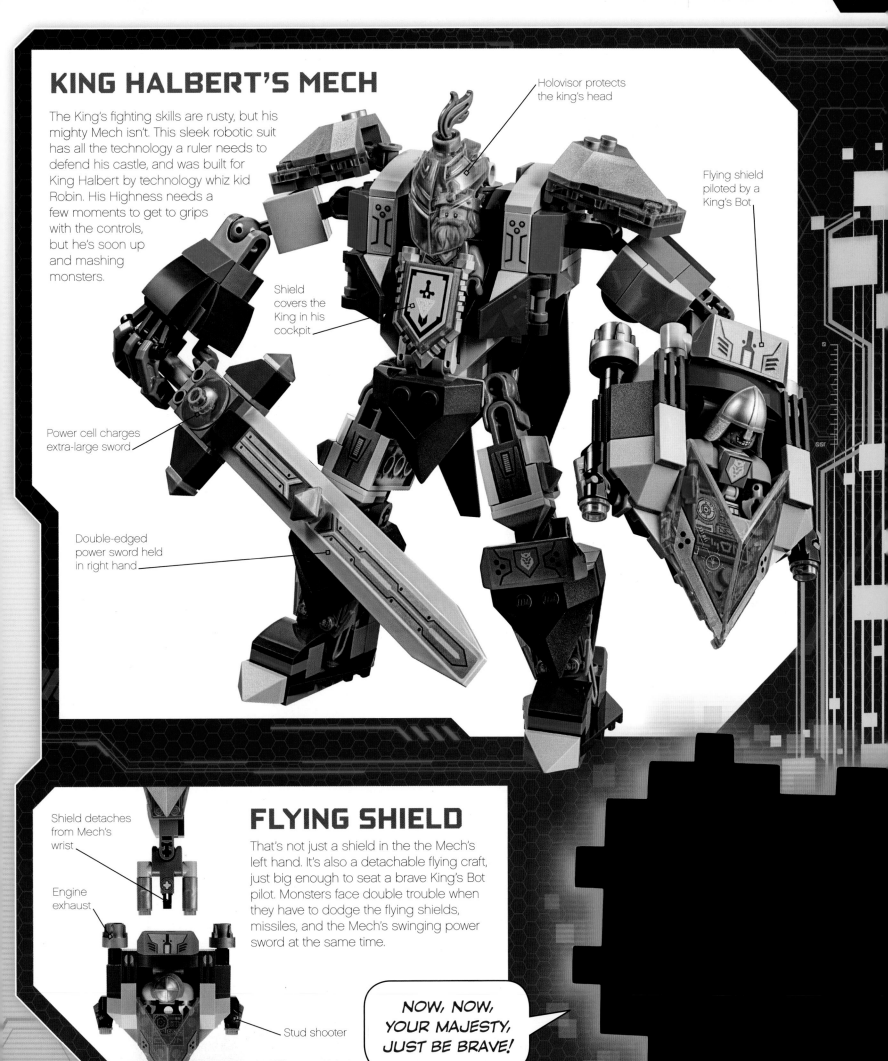

KING HALBERT'S MECH

The King's fighting skills are rusty, but his mighty Mech isn't. This sleek robotic suit has all the technology a ruler needs to defend his castle, and was built for King Halbert by technology whiz kid Robin. His Highness needs a few moments to get to grips with the controls, but he's soon up and mashing monsters.

Holovisor protects the king's head

Flying shield piloted by a King's Bot

Shield covers the King in his cockpit

Power cell charges extra-large sword

Double-edged power sword held in right hand

Shield detaches from Mech's wrist

Engine exhaust

Stud shooter

FLYING SHIELD

That's not just a shield in the the Mech's left hand. It's also a detachable flying craft, just big enough to seat a brave King's Bot pilot. Monsters face double trouble when they have to dodge the flying shields, missiles, and the Mech's swinging power sword at the same time.

NOW, NOW, YOUR MAJESTY, JUST BE BRAVE!

MERLOK'S LIBRARY 2.0

In the topmost tower of King Halbert's castle is the library of the wizard Merlok. It's crammed with strange and fantastical books. But beware! These books are magic, and they are dangerous. That's why the library is always locked—unless there's a power cut.

THE BOOK OF MONSTERS

Here it is... the most obnoxious, spiteful, greedy, two-faced, and just plain evil book in the library. It's stuffed with monsters, and it loves to let them out of its pages to do mean and nasty things.

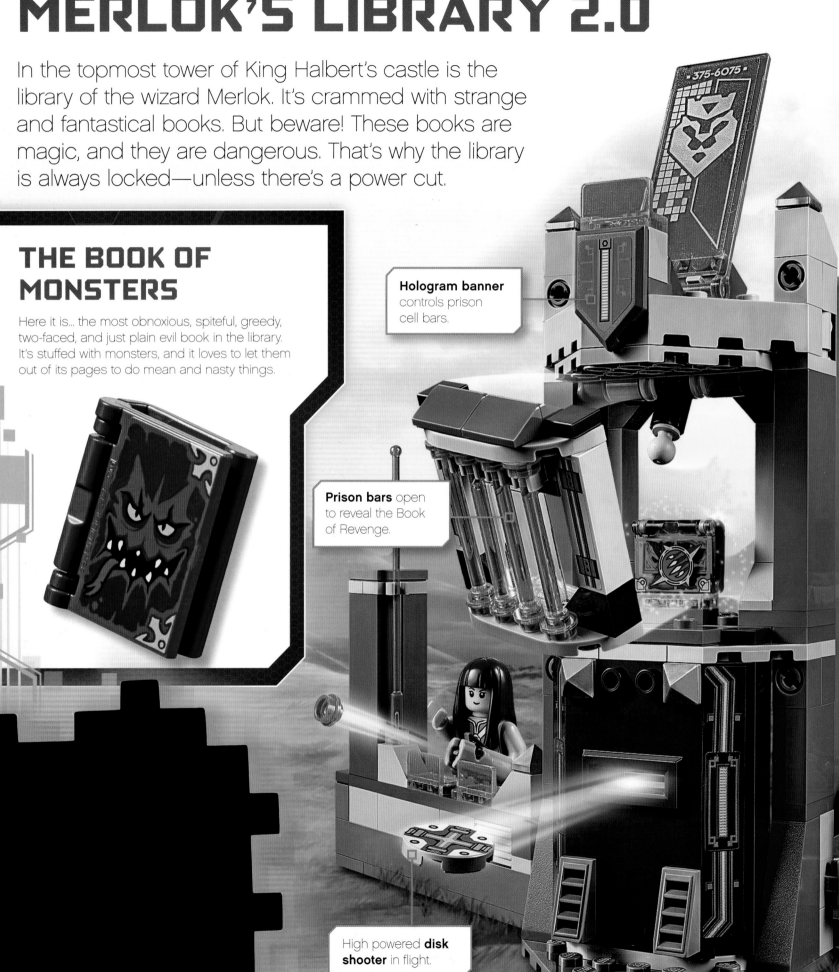

Hologram banner controls prison cell bars.

Prison bars open to reveal the Book of Revenge.

High powered **disk shooter** in flight.

Big Bang

A big magical battle kicks off when Merlok catches Jestro in his library, plotting with the Book of Monsters. Powerful spells crash into each other until the library explodes! This model is Merlok's rebuilt, reinforced, library, for storing all of the lost magical books. Clever Robin built it, and Ava added safety features.

> Translucent **aerial** receives and sends digital messages and picks up on magical energies.

> **Stud shooter** weapon for defending Merlok's new library.

Book of Deception

Book of Revenge

Book of Destruction

Book of Fear

Book of Evil

Book of Chaos

BOOKS OF DARK MAGIC

For years, these evil magic books were safely locked away in Merlok's library. Now they are free, scattered all over Knighton. Can the knights find them before the Book of Monsters swallows them all? If he does, the monsters will become more deceptive, revengeful, destructive, fearsome, evil, and chaotic than ever before.

> I NEED THESE MONSTROUS MAGIC BOOKS BACK... PRONTO!

DATA FILE

SET NUMBER: 70324

PARTS: 288

RELEASED: 2016

MINIFIGURES: 3

ENEMIES OF KNIGHTON

The knights' lives are peaceful, until Jestro the jester goes bad, steals the Book of Monsters, and summons terrifying Magma Monsters to run amok in Knighton! Now the knights must learn how to fight these magical fiery foes—arriving in different (all monstrous) guises.

JESTRO THE JESTER

Jestro wasn't always bad. He was more sad, really. Sad because he felt he was no good at anything. And that's when the Book of Monsters got to him. It convinced him that he would be good— really good—at being evil.

The Book Keeper never speaks— he just grins and bears it

Sometimes you *can* judge a book by its cover

BY THE BOOK

Jestro thinks he is in control of the monster army. In fact, the Book of Monsters more or less tells him what to do. The first monster he makes Jestro summon is the Book Keeper—to carry the demanding Book of Monsters around!

Jestro's insignia and banners feature a jester laughing uncontrollably.

The Evil Mobile
This rolling war wagon is Jestro's answer to the Fortrex. Built by a team of monster mechanics, it has a special fireproof seat— Jestro can't take heat like a monster can!

One of two **transparent catapults**.

Knights must beware the **hidden trap ladder**—it leads to an inner prison!

Giant lava wheels cope with any terrain and can be made to roll faster by inserting globlins into them.

Lower jaw opens and closes as Evil Mobile rolls along.

BAD JOB!

Once, Jestro was bad in a different way. He was bad at his job as the king's jester. So bad, in fact, that people laughed—and not in a good way. He stumbled when he tumbled. He fumbled when he juggled. And when he tried to spin plates—CRASH!

Jestro's magical staff

Dangling skulls on collar

Sparkks, wielding a scythe, tows the Evil Mobile with two chains.

True colors

Since meeting the Book of Monsters, Jestro has really embraced the evil lifestyle. His personality has changed and so too have the colors of his costume—to lava red and poison purple.

DATA FILE

SET NUMBER: 70316

PARTS: 658

RELEASED: 2016

MINIFIGURES: 2

... AND THAT'S WHAT HAPPENS IF YOU FALL INTO BAD COMPANY. OH, JESTRO!

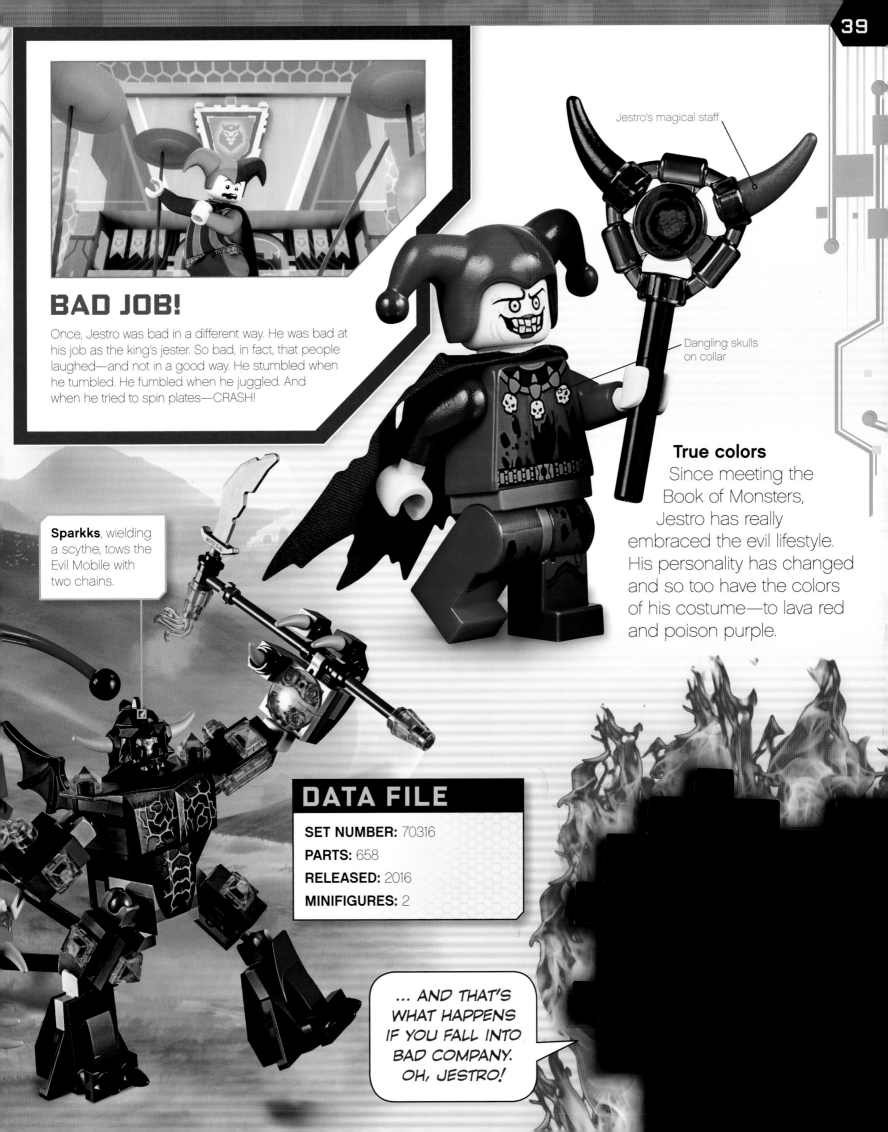

JESTRO'S VOLCANO LAIR

Where does an evil jester go to regroup with his gang between battles? The Volcano Lair, that's where. Located in the Lava Lands, it's the hottest property in Knighton. But don't try to drop in without an invite. Intruders will be caught, questioned, and possibly boiled.

Jestro's **throne** can detach from the top of his lair.

Handle releases trapdoor.

Trapdoor tumbles knights into lava mouth.

DATA FILE

SET NUMBER: 70323
PARTS: 1186
RELEASED: 2016
MINIFIGURES: 10

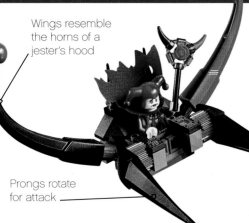

Wings resemble the horns of a jester's hood

Prongs rotate for attack

THRONE UP IN THE AIR

Jestro's throne is also a flying machine. If the knights ever break into the Volcano Lair and try to capture him, he'll simply fly away. So long, knights!

Library hidden behind this wall.

Arrow slit for defending lair.

Spinning lava mouth designed to catch knights who fall through the trapdoor.

IN THE SLAMMER

Knights who take a wrong turn could find themselves trapped when prison walls suddenly slam down around them. They'll just have to cool their heels for a while, until a friend comes to set them free.

DID YOU KNOW?

Jestro's secret library and his Magic Books can only be revealed by pressing a shield, which then collapses a wall.

Lavaria's vehicle hovers over the lair.

Jestro's name burned onto the wall.

Treasure room for storing plundered goods.

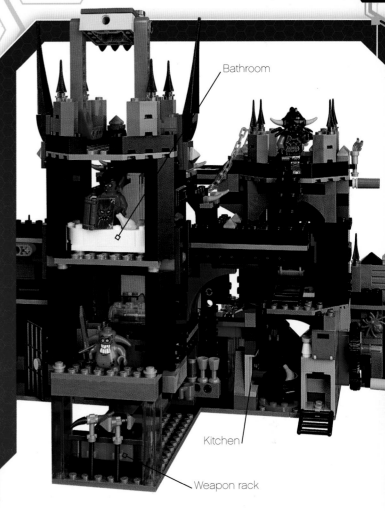

Bathroom

Kitchen

Weapon rack

INSIDE THE LAIR

Modern conveniences abound in the Volcano Lair. There's a bathroom with hot and hotter running water, and a kitchen where monsters can whip up a lava smoothie or pop a pepperoni pizza in the oven. Weapons can be neatly stacked in their rack, and there's always a book around for a bit of evil bedtime reading (head to the library!).

Rotating **saw boobytrap** swings out to block the staircase.

PHEW! IS IT HOT IN HERE? OR AM I COMING DOWN WITH A COMPUTER VIRUS?

Hot Hangout

The Volcano Lair doesn't have air conditioning. It gets pretty hot in there—although it doesn't seem to bother anyone but Jestro.

GENERAL MAGMAR

This monster warlord is the fiercest, smartest, most inspirational leader ever. Or so he says. When he isn't cooking up a battle plan, General Magmar is cooking up Magma Chip Cookies in the kitchen. Too bad they crumble—just like his campaigns.

Longwinded
General Magmar loves to talk. Unfortunately his soldiers don't love his speeches as much as he does.

Big mouthguard for a big mouth

Cape scorched in battle (or in the kitchen)

PRISON BREAK

General Magmar's pride and joy is his terrifying Siege Machine of Doom. This castle-busting convertible is packed with weapons and missiles. It also has a prison. That's at the back, so luckily Clay can NEXO Power his way out while General Magmar's attention is on the battle ahead.

Burning hot **disk launcher** in body of Siege Machine.

Blades demolish brick or stone.

Magma jets burn a path for the vehicle.

General Magmar's **elevated command station** gives him a feeling of power.

DATA FILE

SET NUMBER: 70321

PARTS: 516

RELEASED: 2016

MINIFIGURES: 3

Jaws contain a disk shooter

Two-over-four wheel formation for stability

Cockpit for Flama

Long-range **Globlin catapult**.

SIEGE MACHINE OF DOOM

So you've built an extra high wall around your castle, and now you're safe from monsters. Really? Well, look what happens when General Magmar's Siege Machine of Doom converts to vertical mode. Those monsters will be over your wall and in your face before you can say "Magma Monsters!"

SO MUCH DOOM AND GLOOM WITH THESE MONSTERS —WHAT'S WRONG WITH A SMILE OR TWO?

Ram it Home!

In horizontal mode, the Siege Machine of Doom is a powerful armored vehicle that can be used as a battering ram on wheels. General Magmar commands from the rear, while Flama takes the helm.

Spiked, **flaming hubcap** to deter attackers.

MASSIVE MAGMA MONSTERS

Hot, hotter, and scorching—these three big Magma Monsters should be able to melt a knight's armor in a moment. But when it comes to brain power, they can be more fizzle than sizzle.

Sparkks

Sparkks wants to smash anything he can spy with his great big eye. He's strong enough to do it, too, but those knights just keep outwitting him. Looks like he's in for another telling off from Jestro!

Claws likely to grab another monster by mistake instead of a knight.

Giant **gripping hands** move with pincer motions.

Massively **powerful arms** for swinging weapons.

Infernox

This towering troublemaker hides a nasty secret behind his toothy smile—his gaping mouth is also a prison cell! Infernox has plenty to smile about when he captures Queen Halbert, but his grin turns into a groan when Aaron arrives to rescue the ruler.

Disk shooter hammer

Queen Halbert is upset about being captured!

Prison cell inside jaws

2-in-1 weapon —hammer and spear

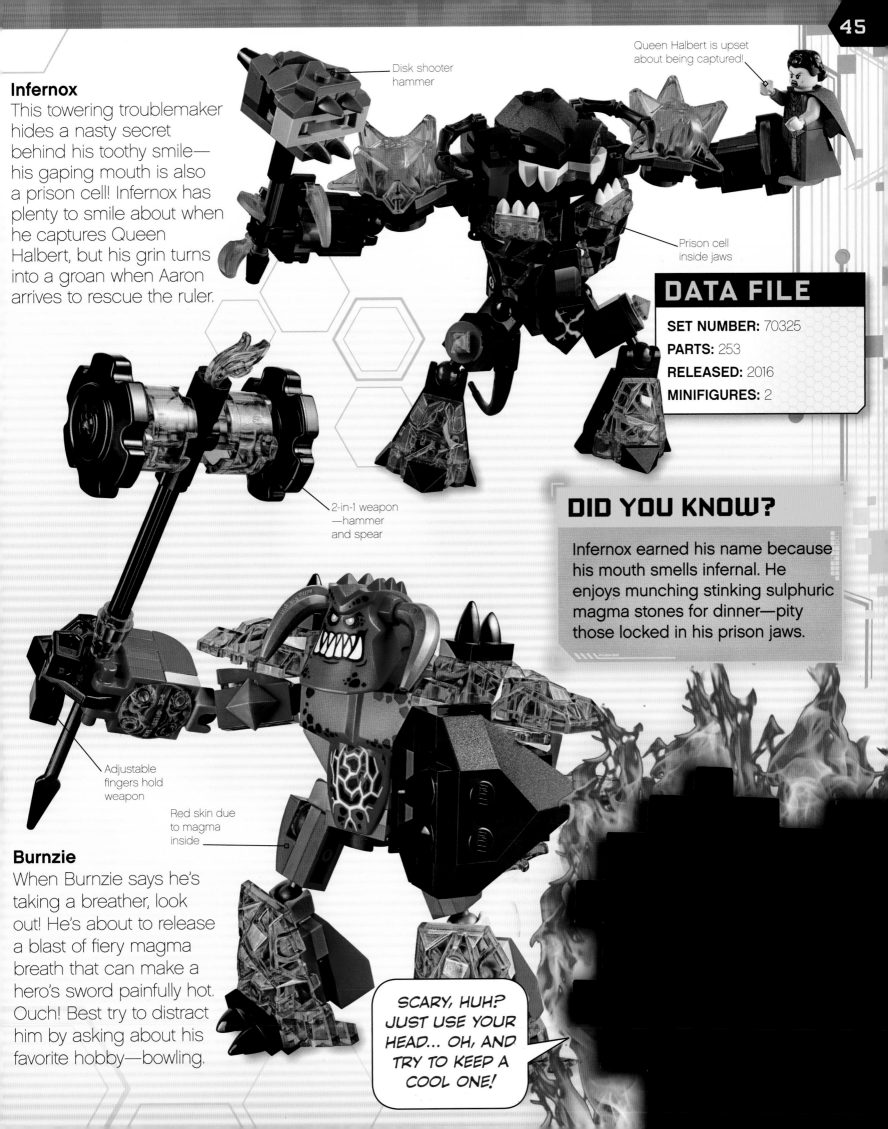

DATA FILE

SET NUMBER: 70325
PARTS: 253
RELEASED: 2016
MINIFIGURES: 2

DID YOU KNOW?

Infernox earned his name because his mouth smells infernal. He enjoys munching stinking sulphuric magma stones for dinner—pity those locked in his prison jaws.

Adjustable fingers hold weapon

Red skin due to magma inside

Burnzie

When Burnzie says he's taking a breather, look out! He's about to release a blast of fiery magma breath that can make a hero's sword painfully hot. Ouch! Best try to distract him by asking about his favorite hobby—bowling.

SCARY, HUH? JUST USE YOUR HEAD... OH, AND TRY TO KEEP A COOL ONE!

MOLTOR AND FLAMA

Together, Moltor and his brother Flama are known as the Hot 'n' Heavy twins. Moltor is rarely far from Flama, and the two often operate together. The Book of Monsters calls this a "2-for-1 deal for destruction!"

DID YOU KNOW?

Moltor and Flama speak to each other using a special rumbling, grumbling language of their own called "Rock Talk." They're probably not saying anything nice!

Spiked shoulder armor

Huge fists made of solid rock

Flama's fiery sword is made of liquid lava like the rest of him

Rock talk

Idle chatter isn't Moltor's thing. He lets his fists do the talking— and they have plenty to say. They are made of giant boulders that can smash, bash, and crash through almost anything. Now that's got to hurt!

Fire helmet protects Flama's head

Too hot to handle

While his brother is all solid rock, Flama is pure molten lava. Don't get too close—he really hates hugs, and he's sure to burn up anything or anyone who gets within touching distance.

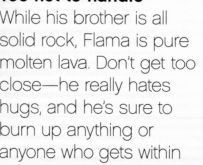

Danger—falling rocks

Moltor's Lava Smasher is guaranteed to make an impact. As it picks up speed, the two massive flaming rocks at the front smash down faster and faster. The road really takes a pounding, and so does anything else unlucky enough to get in the Smasher's way. This doom-dealing vehicle only has room for one, and that's Moltor.

Burning **hot rocks** ensure maximum damage.

Smasher rocks move alternately.

Molten rocks are fired from the in-built catapult.

Jaws scoop up smashed weapons.

FIST BUMP? WITH THESE GUYS? EVEN THE OTHER MONSTERS WON'T DO IT!

High-traction wheel rolls across rocky terrain.

DATA FILE

SET NUMBER: 70313

PARTS: 187

RELEASED: 2016

MINIFIGURES: 2

BEAST MASTER

This tough monster-wrangler is an expert at bringing pesky Globlins and Scurriers into line. Why the eye patch? Some say one of his own Globlins attacked him. But don't let the Beast Master hear you say that.

Snapping jaws gobble up anything in the chariot's path.

Chain gang

Two of the Globlins are so wild that even the Beast Master has trouble controlling them. He has to drag them around on chains. Or are they dragging him?

Chain is checked for weak links regularly

Cross body harness features grumpy Globlin logo

This Globlin has a permanently angry face (his pal is always happy)!

CASTLE ATTACK

Jestro is afraid of the Globlins and Scurriers. They're fierce! So when he needs their help to attack the Royal Castle, he summons the Beast Master from the Book of Monsters to lead the motley crew and the invasion attempt.

Chaos chariot

Stand back—here comes the Chaos Chariot! Towed by two giant Globlins, it lurches along as the Beast Master shouts and hauls on the reins. He is in complete control, of course. He just likes to drive like a maniac!

Globlin **fireball catapult** brings up the rear.

Chain reins for firm control.

Flaming **lava exhaust** spews out flames.

DATA FILE

SET NUMBER: 70314
PARTS: 314
RELEASED: 2016
MINIFIGURES: 2

NOW THAT'S WHAT I CALL A *BEAST* OF A VEHICLE!

GLOBLINS AND SCURRIERS

The monsters Jestro summons come in all shapes and sizes—but all are as pesky as each other. The pear-shaped Scurriers and the bouncing Globlins are capable of great chaos—which is why the Beast Master must be on hand to control them.

Scurrier

Globlins

ASH ATTACKER

This lava soldier is made of volcanic ash, and he scatters it to create a big cloud of trouble. The ash gets in the knights' eyes and up their noses, and can make their vehicles break down, too. Fighting Ash Attacker really can leave you all choked up!

MAGMA CHAINSAW

Like any other chainsaw, Ash Attacker's has a fearsome row of whirring teeth. Unlike any other chainsaw, this one is powered by burning hot magma.

One-handed grip on Magma Blade

FIRESQUITO

Ash Attacker zips into battle in his Firesquito. He's as pesky as an insect that won't go away, buzzing around the knights as he fires flat Globlins, waves his Magma Blade, and scatters ash. Will they or won't they bite the dust?

Flames shooting from exhaust

Batlike wings match black armor.

Winging It

With his jet-black wings, Ash Attacker takes to the air in a cloud of ash. Foes may not spot him until he is right above them!

Silver armor connected by sinister links and chains.

Ash Attacker is a hotshot with his **lava crossbow**.

CRUST SMASHER

He's hard on the outside and soft on the inside—but not in a good way. Crust Smasher's insides are pure molten lava. Punch him, and he'll either punch you back harder with his fist of rock, or burst open and spray you with lava.

Uneven blade shape to cause extra damage.

LAVA SLINGER

Think you can run away? Crust Smasher will be hot on your heels in his speedy Lava Slinger. And with not one but two catapults, those lava missiles are just going to keep on coming.

DATA FILE

SET NUMBER: 70318

PARTS: 442

RELEASED: 2016

MINIFIGURES: 2

Chop, chop!
A strong monster like Crust Smasher has no trouble wielding two weapons. His twin swords are trusty, crusty... but never rusty.

PIE CRUST... PIZZA CRUST... ANYTHING BUT THIS KIND OF CRUST!

CHAOS CATAPULT

The Chaos Catapult flings huge lava rocks that spread panic and confusion wherever they hit. That's Crust Smasher in the jaw-shaped cockpit, taking down fleeing foes with well-aimed bolts from his lava bow.

DATA FILE

SET NUMBER: 70311

PARTS: 93

RELEASED: 2016

MINIFIGURES: 2

LAVARIA

Shhh… keep your lips sealed when Lavaria is around. This silent spy is an expert at gathering enemy secrets to take back to Jestro. Lavaria prefers not to speak. Everything she does is cloaked in secrecy, just like Lavaria herself.

Black cloak for hiding in shadows.

VOLCANO TOPPER

Like a spider, Lavaria scuttles around in the shadows. From this vehicle, normally attached to Jestro's Volcano Lair, she scouts for knights to snatch. Then she operates two grabbing arms with the lever controls.

Pincer arms to grab any seized object—or knight

Stop, thief!
Light-fingered Lavaria will steal anything. Weapons, armor… you name it. If only she could steal a kiss from her beloved Jestro!

Twin hot **lava blades**.

DATA FILE

SET NUMBER: 70318

PARTS: 442

RELEASED: 2016

MINIFIGURES: 2

Body shaped like a giant crossbow.

GLOB LOBBER

Ready, aim, FIRE! Flame Thrower is revving for a burn-up in his lava-powered Glob Lobber. It hurls flaming Globlin-topped missiles, and has scary teeth and claws as well.

FLAME THROWER

If you can't stand the heat, stay away from Flame Thrower. He's made of fire, and shoots flames at foes who venture too close. A dousing with water will put him out, but he'll be back. He just nips back into the Book of Monsters to get reignited.

Burning desire
Setting fire to things is Flame Thrower's idea of fun. The very thought of it makes his face light up. The knights should keep out of his way, or he might light up their vehicles, too.

Massive **mohawk** hairstyle.

Crossbow fired with arrows—stored in quiver worn on Flame Thrower's back.

Serrated saws for extra menace

Advancing teeth and jaws

WILL SOMEONE PLEASE JUST GET ME A BUCKET OF WATER?!

WHIPARELLA

When Whiparella slithers, her victims shiver. One touch from her whips can make them squirm with fear. Whiparella does a lot of squirming herself, too—but with evil, not fear. She's shaped like a big red serpent, and has fangs to match.

Mean expression is Whiparella's happy face—caused by giving someone a good scare!

BORN SCARY

Whiparella was created by the Book of Fear, so no wonder she's scary. Even the Book of Monsters is afraid of her (although he does have a bit of a crush on her too – he thinks she is *beautifully* bad).

Serpent's tail can also lash out like a whip

Magical whips summon the worst fears of whoever they touch

WHIPARELLA'S LAIR

Terrified victims are often dragged into Whiparella's lair, and locked up in the prison. There, she can watch them tremble. The more they tremble, the more she likes it. Only one thing scares Whiparella herself—that's the thought of people not being afraid of her.

Prison bars can bend and move

Dynamite and sharp daggers hidden within lair

Catapult for defending lair from prison breaks

Claw-shaped prison with King's bot inside

Dangerous driver

The ram's skull on Whiparella's Lava Fly vehicle is scary, but not as scary as the driver! Whiparella flicks her whips at anyone she flies by to find out their worst fears.

DATA FILE

SET NUMBER: 70326
PARTS: 530
RELEASED: 2016
MINIFIGURES: 4

Dual control **handlebars**.

Hidden **dagger weapons** on both sides of vehicle.

Low-flying spring-loaded missile punches holes in enemy vehicles.

WANT TO GIVE THE SNAKE LADY A SCARE? JUST CALL HER "WHIMPARELLA!"

ULTIMATE MONSTERS

Thought those monsters were scary before? Now that they have the knights' shields, they're even scarier! The Magma Monsters can't use Merlok's NEXO Powers, but if they hold the shields, then the knights can't use them either!

Ultimate Lavaria

Terrified of tarantulas? Afraid of fanged beasts? Then watch out for Lavaria in Ultimate mode. She'll scuttle right up to you with those pincer-sharp legs—until she's close enough to jab you with either of the sharp ends of her spear.

DID YOU KNOW?

Getting General Magmar's name wrong makes him really angry. Lance's parents joke that he is "General Manager," with bad results.

Scuttling spider legs

Double-bladed spear causes double the trouble

Red-hot flaming sword

Circular saw can be replaced by whirlwind blade if Magmar wants a change

Ultimate General Magmar

Freeze, and do exactly as he says (although freezing might be difficult with all that magma around). This guy likes giving orders, and any knight who disobeys him could end up on the pointy end of those shoulder-mounted circular saws.

Ultimate Beast Master

Clobbered by Globlins. Sucked into a spirit vortex. Blown across the Knighton sky by dynamite. Those are the three possible fates that await anyone running into Beast Master in Ultimate mode. Don't bother trying to decide which is worst. The Beast Master will choose!

Golden chain spins Globlins at frightening speed

Drill dagger

Flame Wreck Hammer

Ultimate Flama

Flama is always fired up for battle, but in Ultimate mode he's really raging. Be sure to dodge that Flame Wreck Hammer when it falls, unless you want to be even more of a hothead than Flama is.

Weapons emit fire as well as crushing blows

JUST WHEN I THOUGHT THAT THINGS COULDN'T GET ANY WORSE...

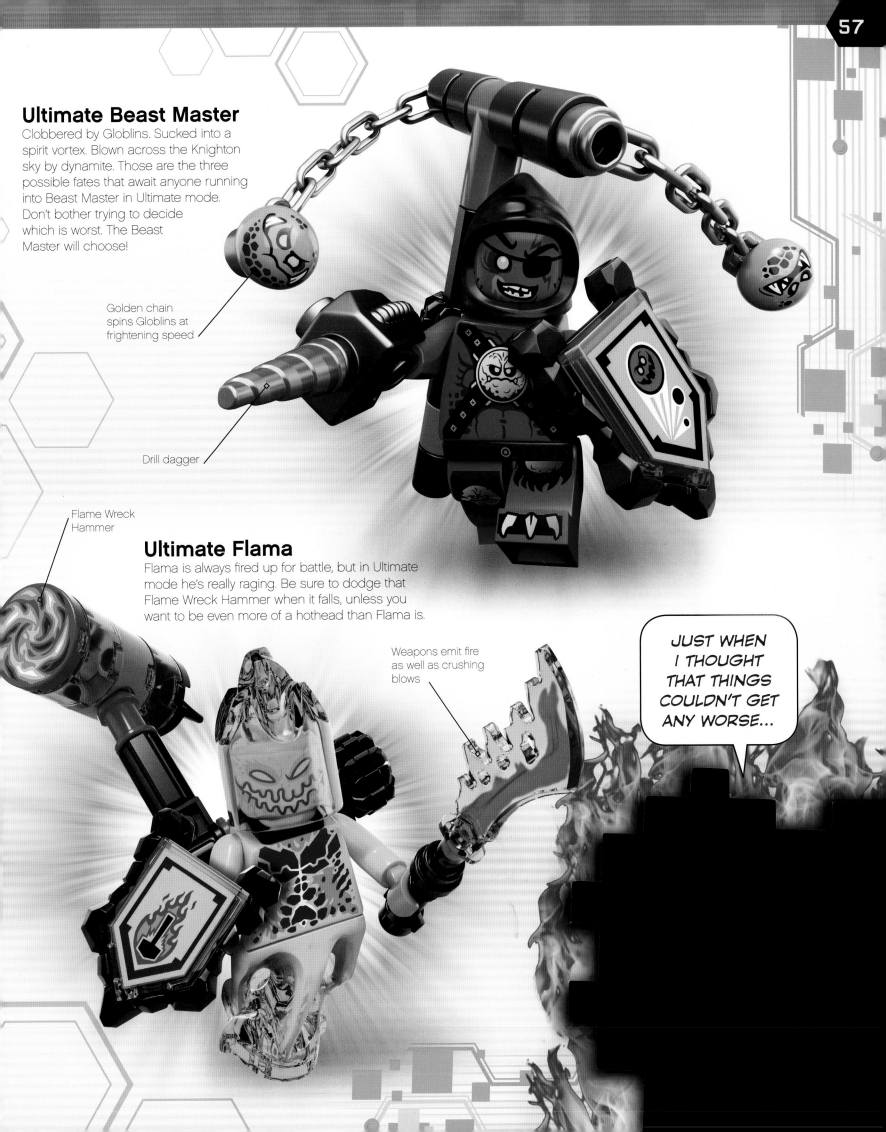

DEFENDING THE KINGDOM

To defeat the monsters invading Knighton, the NEXO KNIGHTS™ heroes must quickly rally together with the soldiers of the land. They also need to download new NEXO Powers from Merlok 2.0 to help banish the fiery brutes back into the Book of Monsters!

THE FORTREX

When Jestro attacks, the knights roll into action in the Fortrex—a huge mobile castle that is also a battle station. Rocks, sand, or swamp are no match for the Fortrex's massive tracks. Look out, monsters—it's on its way!

Holo-banner with royal insignia.

Techalibur sword used to plug in Merlok 2.0.

HIDDEN WEAPON

The drawbridge is up, and all is quiet. A monster might dare to sneak in for a closer look at the Fortrex. Bad move! The hidden disk shooter will fire its missile straight at them.

Rotating stud shooter for rapid firing of missiles.

Clay comes zooming out of the Fortrex on his **Knight Cycle**, normally stored inside.

Lowered drawbridge allows access to knights.

Chef Eclair has his own kitchen inside the Fortrex.

DATA FILE

SET NUMBER: 70317
PARTS: 1140
RELEASED: 2016
MINIFIGURES: 7

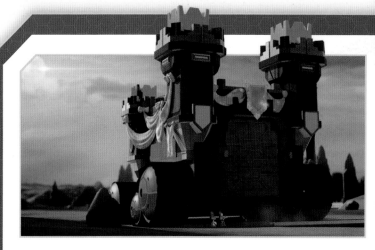

HOME FROM HOME

The heroes live in the Fortrex for a lot of the time, so they are glad it has all the comforts of home. It was originally built for King and Queen Halbert to use when traveling to public appearances all over Knighton, but was remodeled by Ava and Robin to add all the technology that the knights need.

LASER TURRET

Just above each of the Fortrex's rear tracks is a swiveling laser turret. Its twin lasers sweep from side to side, searching for monsters. Woe betide any who get caught in its beams!

ALL ABOARD, KNIGHTS? OK... LET'S ROLL!

Three-wheel front track paired with two wheels at the rear.

Castle keeper

When plugged in and connected, Merlok 2.0 controls the Fortrex. He has been known to lock the knights out if he feels they haven't worked hard enough (or when he forgets the passcode).

INSIDE THE FORTREX

Peek inside the Fortrex, and it's possible to see Merlok 2.0 briefing the knights, Aaron shooting targets in the training area, Axl having a bite in the kitchen, or Clay fixing his Knight Cycle in the repair bay. It's all go!

UP IN THE AIR

The Bowtrex perches on top of the Fortrex. It's a good spot for Aaron to survey the oncoming enemy. Once he's picked his target, he launches himself into the air—then is free to fire on the monsters.

Bowtrex crossbow was invented and installed by Robin.

The Monster Attack Center houses a **monster-targeting rangefinder**.

Dummy target holds sword for practice sessions.

Training target ready and waiting for Aaron in the training arena.

Techno team

Robin and Ava are also based on the Fortrex. Robin works hard in the Invention Lab, and Ava operates the computer system.

Digimagic transmitter keeps the knights connected at all times.

Scurrier locked in **prison cell**.

Winding **chain** lowers the drawbridge.

Control wheel turns the laser turret.

Different **NEXO Powers** can be selected in the Hall of Powers.

The kitchen is fully equipped with **cold and hot taps**, and an oven.

KNIGHTS AT THE ROUND TABLE

Merlok 2.0 calls the knights to the round table to give them their mission instructions. Seats for the knights pop out when Merlok 2.0 takes his place on the table, and fold away again when it's not in use.

HEY... KEEP THAT DRAWBRIDGE RAISED! DON'T LET THE MONSTERS IN!

Shields slot onto backs of chairs at round table.

Clay's Knight Cycle needs some attention in the **repair bay**.

ROYAL SOLDIERS

These loyal soldiers have no NEXO Powers. They fight the monsters using only swords, spears, and pure grit. If they take a bashing, they just get up and carry on. They know that when there's a kingdom to defend, every little helps!

Plain metal sword for hand-to-hand combat.

KEEP CALM AND SOLDIER ON!

Full face helmets come in two styles.

Armor encases soldiers' shoulders and their fronts and backs.

Standard issue **royal pike**.

Royal crest embedded in chestplate.

Keep your head

Just like the knights, the soldiers need head protection, too. These troopers wear either a brimmed helmet or a bucket-shaped helmet.

KNIGHT'S CYCLE

On this swift cycle, a soldier can zip into the heart of battle. Then he can get to work with that lance—maybe poking holes in monsters' vehicles.

Silver lance

DATA FILE

SET NUMBER: 30371

PARTS: 42

RELEASED: 2016

MINIFIGURES: 1

KNIGHTON BATTLE BLASTER

Ready, aim, fire! Then fire again... and again... and again. The Knighton Battle Blaster carries a chest crammed full of disk missiles. This Royal Soldier won't run out of firepower when he has a monster on the run.

Protective windshield

Disk missile launcher lever

Ammo chest

Chopping ax

Double disk shooter

DATA FILE

SET NUMBER: 70310

PARTS: 76

RELEASED: 2016

MINIFIGURES: 2

KNIGHTON HYPER CANNON

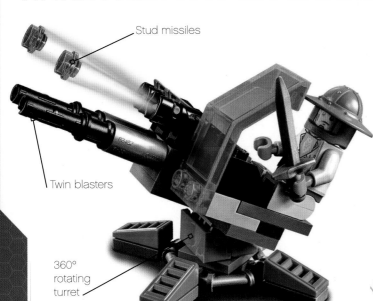

Stud missiles

Twin blasters

360° rotating turret

Royal Soldiers can aim high with this Knighton Hyper Cannon. It rotates on its turret, and tilts up or down. It's equipped with both stud missiles and twin blasters, so multiple hits are guaranteed.

THESE SOLDIERS CAN BE A ROYAL PAIN TO MENACING MONSTERS!

DATA FILE

SET NUMBER: 30373

PARTS: .47

RELEASED: 2016

MINIFIGURES: 1

THE BLACK KNIGHT

There's a new knight in town, and nobody knows who he is. The Black Knight seems young and naïve, and gets into a mess when he tackles the monsters. But he's built himself a cool Robo-Suit, and he's eager to join the knights. Does that sound familiar?

> I'M GOING TO BE KNIGHTON'S "NEXO" TOP KNIGHT!

Chunky dark colored **armor**.

No Peeking!
The Black Knight's helmet hides most of its owner's freckly face. He won't reveal his identity until he has proven himself.

Black-handled sword is bigger than the knight himself!

Shield designed to receive NEXO Powers. This is Foul Steam power—which summons a poisonous fog!

Crossed tool insignia. Is that a hint?

THE BLACK KNIGHT'S MECH

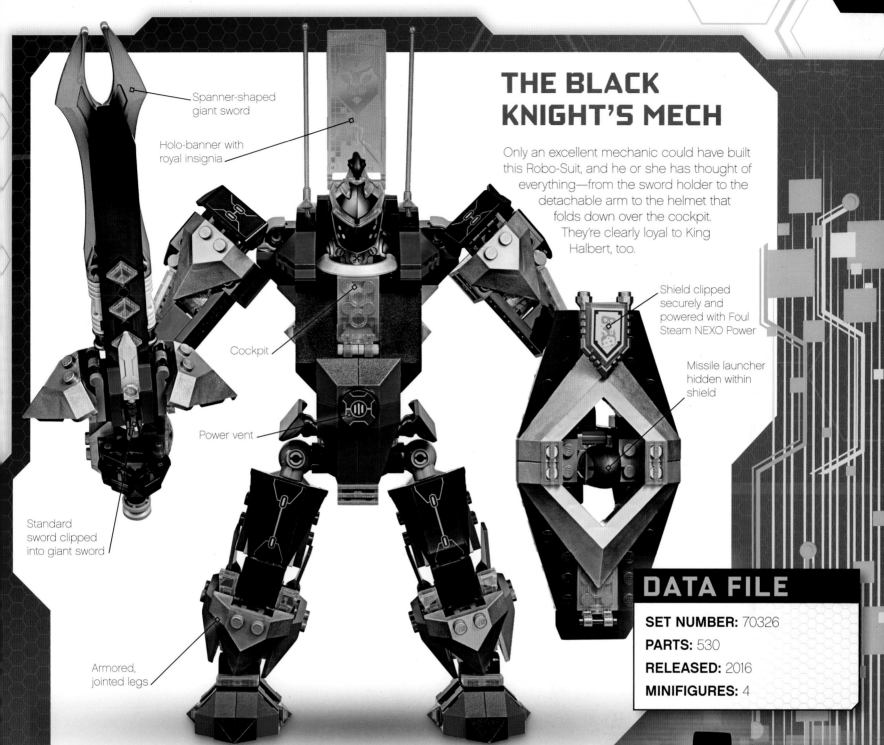

Spanner-shaped giant sword

Holo-banner with royal insignia

Cockpit

Power vent

Standard sword clipped into giant sword

Armored, jointed legs

Shield clipped securely and powered with Foul Steam NEXO Power

Missile launcher hidden within shield

Only an excellent mechanic could have built this Robo-Suit, and he or she has thought of everything—from the sword holder to the detachable arm to the helmet that folds down over the cockpit. They're clearly loyal to King Halbert, too.

DATA FILE

SET NUMBER: 70326
PARTS: 530
RELEASED: 2016
MINIFIGURES: 4

SMALL BUT MIGHTY

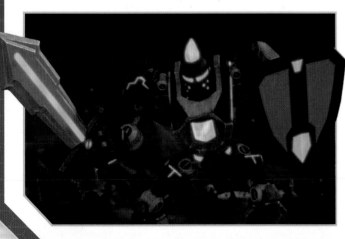

The Black Knight saves the day when some villagers come under attack. The knights are glad of the help—but puzzled by the identity of their rescuer.

WHO IS HE? I'M NOT TELLING. THAT WOULD BE *ROBIN* HIM OF HIS SECRET!

SHIELDS AND POWERS

Thanks to Merlok's new life embedded in Knighton's computer system, and Ava's skills at locating him, the knights have access to greater powers than they ever imagined. Called NEXO Powers, these upgrades give the knights new skills and abilities for fighting the magical monsters.

POWERING UP!

To receive awesome NEXO Powers from Merlok 2.0, the knights raise their shields to the skies. In a flash of light, the powers are then downloaded from the database and the knights are ready for action!

GREATEST HITS

The Greatest Hits NEXO Power allows a knight to mimic another power. Using Greatest Hits can therefore make the knights greater than before! Rolling Fire Ball Power surrounds the user with flames —harmless to them, but dangerous to anyone approaching. With Greatest Hits, a knight might choose to mimic this power against the monsters.

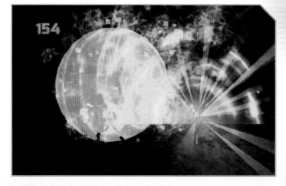

154

NEW NEXO POWER

Explosive Axl

Axl downloads the Ground Power NEXO Power to his shield—and is ready to send a shockwave across the battlefield.

ROCK THROW

Best used at the top of a hill, Rock Throw Power summons a massive boulder to the knights' aid—perfect for rolling over monsters and squashing them flat.

BOMB BLAST

Need to blast a way through some monsters? Use Bomb Blast to clear a path, with a fully charged and fiery explosive device.

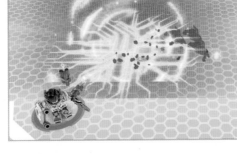

GIANT GROWTH

In a situation where a boost in size and strength is neccessary? Then Giant Growth is just the thing—although the user may become a little clumsier than usual!

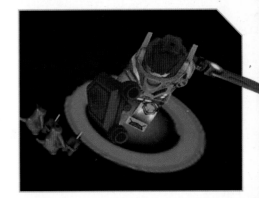

TOXIC STING

This power produces a cloud of noxious gas. Used by a knight, it will send monsters reeling, powerless to defend themselves.

SEE, IT'S A GOOD THING I GOT MYSELF STUCK IN A COMPUTER AFTER ALL!

ULTIMATE KNIGHTS

The knights are always working on new ways to beat Jestro. Smart Robin Underwood has designed bigger, bulkier suits of armor known as Ultimate Armor. They're perfect for bringing down a whole army of Magma Monsters.

Shooter with **six firing barrels**.

Grilled visor to shield Macy's face.

Mace Rain Power summons maces to fall from the sky!

Ultimate Macy

Red is for danger! The Magma Monsters are red, but they'd better watch out because so is Macy's Ultimate Armor. Look out, monsters! You're in danger of being sent flying back into the Book of Monsters by Macy and her power mace.

Ultimate Armor is one color all over— in Macy's case, red.

Dual blades rotate at high speed

Ultimate Clay

In his Ultimate Armor, Clay whips up a whirlwind of power. With four rotating blades, it's enough to make monsters' heads spin and stomachs churn!

Sword Tornado NEXO Power summons two spinning, double-bladed swords.

Orange power points reveal sizzling NEXO Powers

Jetpack with cannons in extended flight mode

Ultimate Lance

Lance takes to the sky in Ultimate Armor with fold-out jet wings. Then he swoops down on the monsters and blasts them with his water cannons. That's the way to dampen their spirits!

THESE SUITS WILL SURELY BRING US *ULTIMATE* VICTORY!

Extended lance with crystal points

Lance wields Take Off Power

ULTIMATE KNIGHTS

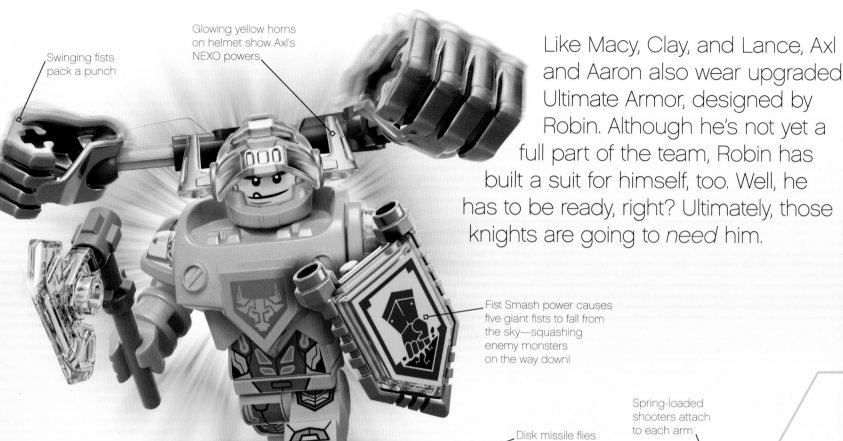

Swinging fists pack a punch

Glowing yellow horns on helmet show Axl's NEXO powers

Like Macy, Clay, and Lance, Axl and Aaron also wear upgraded Ultimate Armor, designed by Robin. Although he's not yet a full part of the team, Robin has built a suit for himself, too. Well, he has to be ready, right? Ultimately, those knights are going to *need* him.

Fist Smash power causes five giant fists to fall from the sky—squashing enemy monsters on the way down!

Spring-loaded shooters attach to each arm

Disk missile flies out of shooter

Ultimate Axl

When Ultimate Axl says he has flying fists, he isn't joking. The mega mitts can detach from his armor, and hurtle toward his foes.

Ultimate Robin

Robin's Ultimate Armor is spring-loaded, providing extra height for this short-legged trainee knight. It also has some of the best upgrades. Well, he did design it himself!

With this Mech Master power-up, Robin can summon Squirebots to his aid

Ultimate Aaron

Exploding onto the battlefield, Ultimate Aaron is ready for the ultimate battle experience. When his arrows start to fly, those monsters really get the point!

In Ultimate mode, Aaron's Blazer Bow is also accompanied by a simpler **compound bow**.

Aaron can summon a volley of poisonous arrows with this **Arrow Strike** power-up.

ROBIN—ALWAYS THERE WHEN YOU NEED HIM!

SET GALLERY

The launch of the LEGO® NEXO KNIGHTS™ theme in 2016 saw the brave knights take on the Magma Monsters in more than 30 sets. How many of these have you collected? Join the battle against Jestro and The Book of Monsters!

70310 Knighton Battle Blaster

70311 Chaos Catapult

70312 Lance's Mecha Horse

70313 Moltor's Lava Smasher

70314 Beast Master's Chaos Chariot

70315 Clay's Rumble Blade

70325 Infernox Captures the Queen

70324 Merlok's Library 2.0

70316 Jestro's Evil Mobile

70327 The King's Mech

30372 Robin's Mini Fortrex

30373 Knighton Hyper Cannon

70317 The Fortrex

70319 Macy's Thunder Mace

70326 The Black Knight Mech

70318 The Glob Lobber

70321 General Magmar's Siege Machine of Doom

70323 Jestro's Volcano Lair

70322 Axl's Tower Carrier

70320 Aaron's Aero Striker V2

70334
Ultimate Beast Master

70335
Ultimate Lavaria

70338
Ultimate General Magmar

70339
Ultimate Flama

70330
Ultimate Clay

70331
Ultimate Macy

70332
Ultimate Aaron

30371 Knight's Cycle

70333
Ultimate Robin

70336
Ultimate Axl

70337
Ultimate Lance

30374 The Lava Slinger

CHARACTER GALLERY

Now that you've met all the key players in the land of Knighton, you should be adept at identifying them in a hurry. In case you are still in any doubt, find them all here—but catch them quick, before they run off again!

Clay

Macy

Lance

Aaron

Axl

Merlok

Merlok 2.0

King Halbert

Queen
Halbert

Ava Prentis

Robin
Underwood

The Black
Knight

Royal Guard

Royal Guard
(no armor)

Royal Guard
(alternative
armor)

Royal
Squire Bot

Lance Bot

Macy Bot

Clay Bot

Axl Bot

Aaron Bot

Chef Eclair

Jestro

The Book of Monsters

The Book Keeper

General Magmar

Lavaria

Beast Master

Moltor

Whiparella

Flama

Ash Attacker

Flame Thrower

Crust Smasher

Globlins

Ultimate Beast Master

Ultimate Lavaria

Ultimate Flama

Ultimate General Magmar

Scurriers

Lava Scurrier

Ultimate Clay

Ultimate Macy

Ultimate Lance

Ultimate Aaron

Ultimate Axl

Ultimate Robin

78

GLOSSARY

Academy
A type of school where people can learn special skills.

Aerodynamic
Having a shape that allows an object to move quickly through the air.

Arsenal
A collection of weapons, or a place where weapons are stored.

Claymore
A very large, double-edged sword.

Graduate
Successfully complete a course of study.

Hologram
A 3D image of someone or something that is not physically present.

Horsepower
A measurement of power—usually relating to a vehicle's engine capacity.

Insignia
A badge belonging to an individual, with a design particular to them alone.

Jester
A servant of a king or queen, whose job is to amuse people.

Lance
A long, thin spear.

Lava
Melted rock that erupts from a volcano.

Mace
A heavy club used as a weapon.

Magma
Melted rock usually found under the Earth's surface.

Mech
A machine or robot operated by controls, for use in battle.

Plunder
Steal goods belonging to someone else.

Squire
A knight's helper.

INDEX

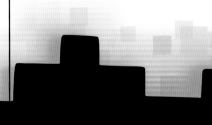

THESE ARE SOME OF MY FAVORITE MAGICAL WORDS!

DK | Penguin Random House

Senior Editor Emma Grange
Project Designer Jon Hall
Design Assistant Stefan Georgiou
Additional Design Rhys Thomas
Pre-Production Producer Marc Staples
Producer Louise Daly
Senior Producer Lloyd Robertson
Editorial Manager Paula Regan
Design Manager Guy Harvey
Art Director Lisa Lanzarini
Publisher Julie Ferris
Publishing Director Simon Beecroft

First American edition, 2016
Published in the United States by DK Publishing
345 Hudson Street, New York, New York 10014

Page design copyright © 2016 Dorling Kindersley Limited
DK, a Division of Penguin Random House LLC
16 17 18 19 10 9 8 7 6 5 4 3 2 1
001—280797—Sept/16

Published in Great Britain by Dorling Kindersley Limited.

A catalog record for this book is available
from the Library of Congress.

ISBN: 978-1-4654-5400-3 (Hardcover)
ISBN 978-1-4654-5478-2 (Library edition)

DK books are available at special discounts when
purchased in bulk for sales promotions, premiums,
fund-raising, or educational use. For details, contact:
DK Publishing Special Markets, 345 Hudson Street,
New York, New York 10014
SpecialSales@dk.com

Printed and bound in China
A WORLD OF IDEAS:
SEE ALL THERE IS TO KNOW

www.dk.com
www.LEGO.com

ACKNOWLEDGMENTS

DK would like to thank Randi Sørensen, Martin Leighton Lindhart, Paul Hansford, Mikkel Lee,
Raphaël Pierre Roger Pretesacque, Samuel Thomas Johnson, Frédéric Roland Andre, Adrian Florea,
Mark John Stafford, Luka Kapeter, Junya Suzuki, Zeina Adly Moawad, and the NEXO KNIGHTS team
at the LEGO Group, Gary Ombler for extra photography, Rosie Peet, Joel Kempson, and Tori Kosara
for extra editorial help, Sam Bartlett for design assistance, and Julia March for her writing.

The Greatest Hits NEXO Power is first
seen in this book. To find out more,
and to scan it, turn to page 68.